Arkansas

A Buddy Book
by
Julie Murray

ABDO
Publishing Company

VISIT US AT
www.abdopub.com

Published by ABDO Publishing Company, 4940 Viking Drive, Edina, Minnesota 55435.

Printed in the United States.

Edited by: Sarah Tieck
Contributing Editor: Michael P. Goecke
Graphic Design: Deb Coldiron, Maria Hosley
Image Research: Sarah Tieck
Photographs: clipart.com, Digital Vision, Getty Images, One Mile Up, PhotoDisc, Photos.com

Library of Congress Cataloging-in-Publication Data

Murray, Julie, 1969-
    Arkansas / Julie Murray.
        p. cm. — (The United States)
    Includes bibliographical references (p.   ) and index.
    ISBN 1-59197-663-4
    1. Arkansas—Juvenile literature. I. Title II. Series: Murray, Julie, 1969- . United
States

F411.3.M87 2005
976.7—dc22

                                                        2004045087

Table Of Contents

A Snapshot Of Arkansas

The state of Arkansas has many natural areas. There are rivers, natural springs, mountains, and plains. This state is special because it has many different natural places. This is why Arkansas is called "The Natural State."

There are 50 states in the United States. Every state is different. Every state has an official state nickname.

Arkansas has 51 state parks, three national forests, a national river, and a national park.

Arkansas became the 25th state on June 15, 1836. The United States bought the land from France as part of the Louisiana Purchase.

Arkansas has about 53,183 square miles (137,743 sq km) of land. It is the 27th-largest state in the United States.

President Thomas Jefferson helped buy the Louisiana Territory from France in 1803.

Where Is Arkansas?

There are four parts of the United States. Each part is called a region. Each region is in a different area of the country. The United States Census Bureau says the four regions are the Northeast, the South, the Midwest, and the West.

Arkansas is in the South region. The weather in this part of the United States is warm and humid. Sometimes it gets very hot.

Four Regions of the United States of America

ALASKA

WASHINGTON

MONTANA

NORTH DAKOTA

OREGON

IDAHO

MINNESOTA

WISCONSIN

MICHIGAN

VERMONT

MAINE

NEW
HAMPSHIRE

MASSACHUSETTS

NEW
YORK

RHODE ISLAND

CONNECTICUT

WYOMING

SOUTH DAKOTA

NEVADA

UTAH

COLORADO

NEBRASKA

IOWA

ILLINOIS

INDIANA

OHIO

PENNSYLVANIA

NEW JERSEY

DELAWARE

Washington D.C.

MARYLAND

CALIFORNIA

KANSAS

MISSOURI

WEST
VIRGINIA

VIRGINIA

KENTUCKY

ARIZONA

NEW MEXICO

OKLAHOMA

ARKANSAS

TENNESSEE

NORTH CAROLINA

SOUTH
CAROLINA

MISSISSIPPI

ALABAMA

GEORGIA

TEXAS

LOUISIANA

FLORIDA

HAWAII

West

Midwest

South

Northeast

Arkansas is bordered by six other states. Missouri is north. Oklahoma and Texas are on the western side. Louisiana is on the southern border. Tennessee and Mississippi are to the east.

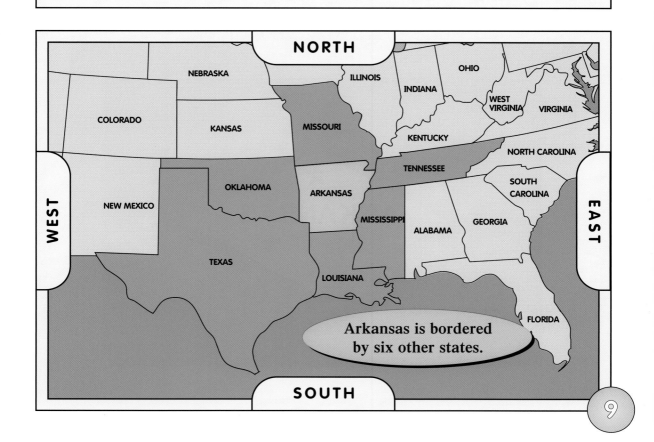

Arkansas is bordered by six other states.

Arkansas

State abbreviation: AR

State nickname: The Natural State

State capital: Little Rock

State motto: *Regnat populus* (Latin for "The people rule")

Statehood: June 15, 1836, 25th state

State flag:
Adopted in 1924

ARKANSAS

Population: 2,673,400, ranks 33rd

Land area: 53,183 square miles (137,743 sq km), ranks 27th

State tree: Pine

State song: "Arkansas"

State government: Three branches: legislative, executive, and judicial

Average July temperature: 81°F (27°C)

Average January temperature: 40°F (4°C)

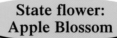
State flower:
Apple Blossom

State animal:
White-tailed Deer

State bird:
Mockingbird

Cities And The Capital

Little Rock is the largest city in the state. More than 180,000 people live in Little Rock. Many Little Rock residents grow flowers. The city's nickname is "City of Roses."

The night skyline of Little Rock.

Little Rock is located in the middle of Arkansas. It is on the shores of the Arkansas River.

The city was named by Bernard de La Harpe in 1722. He was a French explorer who came to Arkansas in search of a green emerald. Instead he found small bluffs by the Arkansas River. The rocky bluffs became a landmark. La Harpe called the area "La Petite Roche." This means "Little Rock."

Little Rock is also the capital of Arkansas. This means that the state government is located here. Government leaders meet at the state capitol building. This building looks like the United States Capitol in Washington, D.C. But, it is much smaller.

The state capitol building in Little Rock, Arkansas.

Famous Citizens

William Jefferson "Bill" Clinton (1946-)

Bill Clinton is one of the most famous people who have called Arkansas home. Clinton was president of the United States from 1993 to 2001. He was the 42nd president of the United States. He was born in Hope and grew up in Hot Springs. Before becoming president, Bill Clinton was governor of Arkansas for 12 years. At 32 years old, he was one of the youngest Americans ever elected governor.

President Bill Clinton

Famous Citizens

Maya Angelou (1928-)

Maya Angelou was born in St. Louis, Missouri. She grew up in Stamps, Arkansas. She is an author and an actress. Angelou was nominated for an award for the part she played in a television movie called Roots. She is also known for her book, *I Know Why the Caged Bird Sings*. This book tells of her childhood in Arkansas.

Maya Angelou

The Ozarks

The Ozarks is an area of land in northwestern Arkansas. The Ozarks are covered with rugged land and thick forests. There are mountains and high plateaus. Deep valleys have been formed by rivers.

There are more than 2,000 limestone caves in the Ozarks. Some of the caves are millions of years old. Blanchard Springs Caverns has many caves to explore. There is even an underground river. Rock formations such as stalagmites and stalactites are found here.

Stalactites hang from the ceilings of caves.

Stalagmites form on cave floors.

Some of the first people to live in Arkansas thousands of years ago lived in the Ozarks. They made their homes in caves and under rock cliffs. These people were called bluff dwellers.

The Ozarks are also known for natural cold springs. A cold spring forms when water bubbles up from the ground. The water forms large pools. Mammoth Springs is a cold spring. It is among the largest natural springs in the country.

People visit the Ozarks to see the natural landscape.

The Mississippi Delta

The Mississippi River's alluvial plain covers the eastern part of Arkansas. This land is also called the Mississippi Delta.

The Mississippi Delta has flat farmland and swampy bayous. The flooding of the Mississippi and Arkansas rivers over time made this land very fertile. This means it is an ideal place to grow crops.

Many people who live in the Mississippi Delta are farmers. The farmers here grow rice, soybeans, cotton, wheat, and corn. Arkansas is the number one producer of rice in the United States.

Rice is a crop grown in swampy areas like this.

The Mississippi Delta is flat land except for a 150-mile (241-km) stretch of land called Crowley's Ridge. This narrow strip of land rises more than 250 feet (76 m). It stands out against the flat lands of the Mississippi Delta. Crowley's Ridge is a great place for outdoor activities. Hiking, biking, camping, fishing, and swimming are all enjoyed in this area.

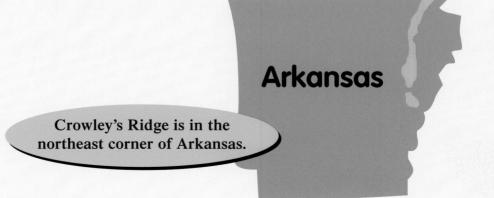

Arkansas

Crowley's Ridge is in the northeast corner of Arkansas.

Hot Springs

Hot Springs National Park is located in the Ouachita Mountain area in western Arkansas.

In Hot Springs, water bubbles out of the earth. It is about 143° Fahrenheit (62°C). People go there to help themselves feel better. Many people say that the natural hot springs have healing powers.

Steam rises from a hot spring.

Arkansas

1541: Hernando de Soto arrives in Arkansas. He is the first European in Arkansas.

The Louisiana Purchase

1803: President Thomas Jefferson makes a deal for the United States to buy Arkansas in the Louisiana Purchase from France.

1836: Arkansas becomes the 25th state of the United States on June 15.

1842: The first state capitol is completed in Little Rock. It is called the Old State House.

1861: Arkansas leaves the United States to become part of the Confederate States of America. This is a group of southern states that fought in the United States Civil War.

1868: Arkansas rejoins the United States.

1921: Oil is discovered near a small town called El Dorado.

1932: Arkansas elects the first female United States senator. Her name was Hattie Wyatt Caraway. She was the state's representative from 1932 to 1945.

1992: Bill Clinton is elected president of the United States.

2004: The William J. Clinton Presidential Library opens in Little Rock.

Fireworks were part of the opening of the Clinton Presidential Library.

Cities in Arkansas

Fort Smith

★ Little Rock

Hot Springs

Pine Bluff

Hope

Texarkana

Stamps

El Dorado

Important Words

alluvial land that has extra minerals because of flooding.

bayou a marshy inlet of a lake or river.

fertile land that is healthy and able to grow many crops.

humid air that is damp or moist.

Louisiana Purchase a deal that allowed the United States to buy land from France. Part of this land later became Arkansas.

nickname a name that describes something special about a person or a place.

plateau a flat-topped mountain.

Web Sites

To learn more about Arkansas, visit ABDO Publishing Company on the World Wide Web. Web site links about Arkansas are featured on our Book Links page. These links are routinely monitored and updated to provide the most current information available.

www.abdopub.com

Index